100

THINGS TO DO IN

MADISON

BEFORE YOU

DIE

100

THINGS TO DO IN

MADISON
BEFORE YOU
DIE

KATIE VAUGHN

Library of Congress Control Number: 2016955741
ISBN: 9781681060835

Design by Jill Halpin
Cover Image: Gregg Schieve

Printed in the United States of America
17 18 19 20 21   5 4 3 2 1

Please note that websites, phone numbers, addresses, and company names are subject to change or cancellation. We did our best to relay the most accurate information available, but due to circumstances beyond our control, please do not hold us liable for misinformation. When exploring new destinations, please do your homework before you go.

DEDICATION

To Will, Olivia, and Dylan, who make Madison home.

· ·

CONTENTS

• •

Music and Entertainment

• •

Sports and Recreation

Culture and History

• •

Shopping and Fashion

PREFACE

If you're reading this book, you've likely heard of or experienced for yourself the magical mash-up that is Madison, Wisconsin. A place where Midwestern down-to-earthness meets progressive thought and independent spirit. Where what was once farmland and forest is now fertile ground for artistic expression and entrepreneurial innovation. Where traditions are fiercely protected while simultaneously being treated to fresh interpretations. Where the Ironman coexists with cheese curds.

Since I grew up in the area, I paused before attending the University of Wisconsin-Madison. Would it be any different from what I'd known all my life? But going to college here, then leaving the state for graduate school and my first few jobs, and returning to put down roots and start a family taught me an important lesson about Madison: The city meets you where you're at. Campus is its own ever-changing ecosystem, while young professionals find an exciting scene that evolves with them. Adults of all ages can enjoy the city's restaurants, bars, music venues, galleries, festivals, sporting events, parks, and trails. And it's hard to imagine a better place to be a kid.

Madison isn't perfect. But it's filled with smart, passionate people working hard every day to overcome differences, end disparities, and make the city a place where everyone can live their best life.

• •

The biggest challenge in writing this book was choosing only 100 elements to highlight. One could write a 100-things book just about Madison's dining scene—heck, just its beer scene—or cultural landscape, or all the neat things happening in the suburbs. I hope you'll consider this book a starting point for exploring this exciting and eclectic city, digging a little deeper, or finding new parts to love.

I'd love to hear about your experiences. Find me on Twitter at @katiemv, or follow the book at @100ThingsMadison on Facebook, and tag your own #100ThingsMadison adventures.

Katie Vaughn

ACKNOWLEDGMENTS

A huge thanks to Judy Frankel, Shayna Mace, and Shanna Wolf; to Rick and Sue Zimmerman and Nikki Carrico; and to my friends, colleagues, old classmates, and Facebook friends who were incredibly generous with ideas, insights, access, and opportunities, and who continue to bring the city to life.

Photo Credit: Joey Reuteman

Photo Credit: Emily Mills

FOOD AND DRINK

EAT LOCAL
AT THE DANE COUNTY FARMERS' MARKET

High on nearly every list of Madison must-dos is the Dane County Farmers' Market, and a stroll around the Capitol Square on a sunny Saturday morning will easily show you why. The largest producer-only farmers' market in the country, going strong since 1972, brings more than 160 vendors each week from spring through fall to sell veggies, cheese, meat, honey, flowers, and other locally made goodies. You might rub elbows with the city's best chefs, who regularly shop the local markets for the freshest ingredients for their farm-to-table dishes, and you'll certainly get to chat with the farmers, growers, and producers who make the most of Wisconsin's agricultural riches. Do not leave without bags of cheese curds, cheesy bread, or preferably both.

Held on Saturdays on the Capitol Square from April to November.
(An indoor market is held in the winter.)
(608) 455-1999, dcfm.org

TIP
For the best selection and smallest crowds, arrive as close to the 6:15 a.m. opening as possible. By mid-morning in the summer, the Square is packed with shoppers.

SAY CHEESE CURD!

In the Dairy State, no food is celebrated as enthusiastically as the cheese curd. What the heck is a cheese curd? Simply put, it's a byproduct that's set aside when cheddar gets molded into blocks to age. But this explanation does little to convey the absolute deliciousness of these small, slightly salty, squeaky morsels. Eat 'em fresh and cold, or try them in the rendition that's become a local delicacy: deep-fried in batter, which is often made with a local beer. Bars and county fairs have served up fried cheese curds for decades. More recently, the city's coolest restaurants have added them to their menus, offering them with the traditional ranch and more adventurous dipping sauces, and inspiring diners to embark on taste-testing tours.

Here are just a few of the places—all within walking distance of one another—that make stellar deep-fried cheese curds:

The Old Fashioned
23 N. Pinckney St., (608) 310-4545
theoldfashioned.com

Graze
1 S. Pinckney St., (608) 251-2700
grazemadison.com

Tipsy Cow
102 King St., (608) 287-1455
tipsycowmadison.com

Merchant
121 S. Pinckney St., (608) 259-9799
merchantmadison.com

GET THE BOOT
AT THE ESSEN HAUS

The Essen Haus is everything you'd expect a German-themed restaurant to be: beer steins hang above the wood bar, schnitzel dominates the dinner menu, staffers dress in dirndls and lederhosen, and bands get diners dancing to oompah music most nights of the week. The party's been going on for more than 30 years, with 16 rotating German biers on tap inspiring patrons to drink from Das Boot. It's a rite of passage to share the two-liter boot-shaped glass with your tablemates. The most jovial of drinking games has you sipping and then passing the boot around—no setting it back on the table, the official rules state—until the beer is gone. Afterward, a spin out on the dance floor is a no-brainer.

514 E. Wilson St., (608) 255-4674
essen-haus.com

APPRECIATE THE CRAFT
OF THE COCKTAIL
AT MERCHANT

Merchant is known for bringing the craft cocktail craze to Madison back in 2010. Yet the downtown restaurant should also be credited with turning what could have been a passing fad into the gold standard for concocting a quality drink. Inspired by the late-19th-century sense of craft, the cool farm-to-table eatery shifts gears with the changing seasons, and the approach extends to its cocktail offerings, which make use of 100-plus whiskeys and more than 20 types of gin, tequila, and rum. Perusing the extensive cocktail list is an experience—nearly every offering on the 60-page menu comes with a backstory—but a worthy endeavor, especially when it leads you to a gem like The Regret, an herby mix of lime juice, rosemary, and gin or vodka.

121 S. Pinckney St., (608) 259-9799
merchantmadison.com

MAKE EATING
AN EVENT

The one thing Madison likes more than local food is an event devoted to local food. Taste of Madison is the granddaddy experience, highlighting specialties from more than 80 restaurants. The centerpiece of the Mad City Vegan Fest is a food court with plant-based treats, while SloPig celebrates the heritage pork movement with a celebrity chef competition. The hip Yum Yum Fest brings together two dozen of the city's hottest eateries in a bash organized by the Madison Area Chefs Network. The collective also organizes MACN Chef Week with special events, kitchen takeovers, and competitions. And twice a year, *Madison Magazine* presents Restaurant Week, in which 50 of the area's finest restaurants offer special three-course dinner (and some lunch) menus. Dig in!

Taste of Madison is held Labor Day weekend on the Capitol Square.
tasteofmadison.com

Mad City Vegan Fest occurs in June at the Alliant Energy Center.
veganfest.org

SloPig is held in the spring.
slopig.com

Yum Yum Fest takes place in August at Central Park.
yumyumfest.org

MACN Chef Week is in March.
isthmus.com/chefweek

***Madison Magazine*'s Restaurant Week is held in both January and July.**
madisonrestaurantweek.com

TAP INTO
THE LOCAL BEER SCENE

Local beer rocks! The New Glarus Brewing Company, the Great Dane, and Capital Brewery are the pioneers who've paved the way for smaller, more experimental breweries such as Ale Asylum, Karben4, Next Door Brewing, One Barrel Brewing, and the Wisconsin Brewing Company, to name just a few. So many fantastic options make a beer fest an efficient—and fun—way to sample. The Great Taste of the Midwest showcases more than 150 Midwest brewers, while the Quivey's Grove Beer Fest serves up 100 brews. The New Glarus Oktoberfest is legendary, and the *Isthmus* OktoBEERfest puts a hip spin on the tradition. Last but not least, Madison Craft Beer Week packs in tours, classes, dinners, and plenty of local suds in a celebration that happily stretches for 10 days.

The Great Taste of the Midwest takes place in August.
greattaste.org

The Quivey's Grove Beer Fest is held in October.
quiveysgrove.com

New Glarus Oktoberfest is held the last weekend of September.
swisstown.com

The *Isthmus* OktoBEERfest takes place in late September.
isthmusoktobeerfest.com

Madison Craft Beer Week is held in late April and early May.
isthmus.com/madison-craft-beer-week

New Glarus Brewing Company
2400 WI-69, New Glarus, (608) 527-5850
newglarusbrewing.com

Great Dane Pub & Brewing Co.
123 E. Doty St., (608) 284-0000
876 Jupiter Dr., (608) 442-1333
357 Price Pl., (608) 661-9400
2980 Cahill Main, Fitchburg, (608) 442-9000
greatdanepub.com

Capital Brewery
7734 Terrace Ave., Middleton, (608) 836-7100
capitalbrewery.com

Ale Asylum
2002 Pankratz St., (608) 663-3926
aleasylum.com

Karben4 Brewing
3698 Kinsman Blvd., (608) 241-4812
karben4.com

Next Door Brewing Company
2439 Atwood Ave., (608) 729-3683
nextdoorbrewing.com

One Barrel Brewing Company
2001 Atwood Ave., (608) 630-9286
onebarrelbrewing.com

Wisconsin Brewing Co.
1079 American Way, Verona, (608) 848-1079
wisconsinbrewingcompany.com

ENJOY A
MOVEABLE FEAST

A delightful sign of spring is the reemergence of the city's beloved food carts. Library Mall and the Capitol Square, which bookend State Street, boast the densest collections of colorful trucks serving up flavors of Peru, Indonesia, Costa Rica, Thailand, Greece, and beyond. Choose among falafel, empanadas, Korean tacos, spicy tofu buns, cheese curds, and tater tots. While mobile restaurants are popular across the country, they're more than a foodie fad in Madison. The city has regulated food carts since the late 1970s and even employs a street vending coordinator. Let's Eat Out!, a coalition of independently owned carts, coordinates dinners across the Madison area, while *Isthmus,* the city's alt-weekly newspaper, hosts a Food Cart Fest each spring with about 40 carts doling out dishes at a downtown park.

LET TORY MILLER
COOK DINNER

What do the city's finest French restaurant, a farm-to-table gastropub, a small-plates eatery, and a sleek pan-Asian joint have in common? L'Etoile, Graze, Estrellón, and Sujeo all showcase the tastes and talents of chef Tory Miller. Born in South Korea and raised in Racine, Wisconsin, the mohawked Miller is renowned for the creative and delicious ways he melds influences—from his French training and experiences working in major New York kitchens to favorite dishes from his childhood and travels to a passion for highlighting local ingredients. And it's not just local diners who have taken notice. Miller was one of 20 semifinalists nationally for the 2016 James Beard Award for outstanding chef and he took home the Best Chef: Midwest title in 2012.

L'Etoile, 1 S. Pinckney St., (608) 251-0500
letoile-restaurant.com

Graze, 1 S. Pinckney St., (608) 251-2700
grazemadison.com

Estrellón, 313 W. Johnson St., (608) 251-2111
estrellonrestaurant.com

Sujeo, 10 N. Livingston St., (608) 630-9400
sujeomadison.com

EXPAND YOUR PIZZA
POSSIBILITIES AT IAN'S

Four words: mac n' cheese pizza. If this sounds like an idea hatched after a long night of "studying" back in college, you're not far from the truth. With a dream of creating a by-the-slice pizza place, Ian Gurfield toured college towns before opening the first Ian's Pizza near the University of Wisconsin-Madison campus in 2001. Crazy-creative pies like chipotle sweet potato, buffalo chicken, and mac n' cheese—still the top seller—attracted hungry college kids and serious foodies alike, prompting a second restaurant to open just four years later. Today, pizza lovers try out monthly specials like drunken ravioli, chili cheese frito, eggplant pesto, and chicken pot pie pies and take comfort in knowing they can now get their Ian's fix in Milwaukee, Denver, and Seattle, too.

100 State St., (608) 257-9248
319 N. Frances St., (608) 257-9248
ianspizza.com

GIVE A FISH FRY A TRY

Wisconsinites look forward to Fridays not just as the gateway to the weekend, but because it brings about a weekly delicacy: the fish fry. The Catholic requirement of abstaining from meat on Fridays combined with taverns serving food during Prohibition created a culinary tradition that just won't quit. And who'd want it to? Cod, walleye, perch, or bluegill, first beer-battered or breaded and then fried, is delicious. And when it's offered up with coleslaw and fries or a baked potato—and don't forget a chilly brew or brandy old fashioned—you've got yourself a meal and a quintessentially Wisconsin one at that. Practically every restaurant and bar in town has a Friday fish fry special, but taverns and supper clubs are the real catches.

SAMPLE GLOBAL FLAVORS
ON PARK STREET

If you crave cuisine from around the world, set your GPS to Park Street. This thoroughfare connecting the south side to downtown is home to restaurants representing tastes from Mexico to China to India. Choose among authentic tacos and tortas at Taqueria Guadalajara, El Pastor, and Sol Azteca Fusion Food, or build your own burrito or quesadilla at El Rancho Mexican Grill. Satisfy a hankering for Chinese comfort food at Ichiban Sichuan, Jade Garden, Orient House, or Mini Hot Pot. Opt for Japanese fare at Edo or Ramen Station, or get dessert (and much more) at Asian Sweet Bakery. You can dig into Indian specialties at Taj or explore Cambodian dishes at Angkor Wat, the newest addition to the lineup of international eateries.

Taqueria Guadalajara, 1033 S. Park St.
(608) 250-1824, lataqueriaguadalajara.com

El Pastor Mexican Restaurant, 2010 S. Park St.
(608) 280-8898, elpastorcatering.com

El Rancho Mexican Grill, 819 S. Park St.
(608) 284-9702, el-rancho-mexican-grill.letseat.at

Sol Azteca Fusion Food, 1821 S. Park St.
(608) 819-8779, solaztecafusiongrill.eat24hour.com

Ichiban Sichuan, 610 S. Park St.
(608) 819-8808, ichibanmadison.com

Jade Garden, 1109 S. Park St.
(608) 260-9890, jadegardenmadison.com

Orient House Chinese Restaurant, 626 S. Park St.
(608) 373-5316, orienthousewi.com

Mini Hot Pot, 1272 S. Park St.
(608) 709-6558, facebook.com/MiniHotPotMadison

Edo Japanese Restaurant, 532 S. Park St.
(608) 268-0247, edojapanesemadison.com

Ramen Station, 1124 S. Park St.
(608) 819-8918, ramenstationmadison.com

Asian Sweet Bakery, 1017 S. Park St.
(608) 665-2988

Taj Indian, 1256 S. Park St.
(608) 268-0772, taj-madison.com

Angkor Wat, Khmer and Thai Cuisine
602 S. Park St., (608) 442-5666

HAVE SOME WINE TIME

Wisconsin's harsh weather isn't ideal for growing grapes, but that hasn't stopped a handful of area wineries from producing some easy-sipping vino. At the historic Wollersheim Winery in beautiful Prairie du Sac, sample reds, whites, ports, the super-popular semi-dry white Prairie Fumé, and, if you're lucky, Ice Wine, a sweet local specialty made with grapes frozen on the vine. Out west in Barneveld, Botham Vineyards offers tours and tastes during the warmer months; mark your calendar for its Vintage Celebration, which pairs wines with classic cars each August. Or tuck into Toot + Kate's, a self-serve wine bar in a couldn't-be-cuter space on Verona's Main Street.

Wollersheim Winery and Distillery
7876 WI-88, Prairie du Sac
(608) 643-6515
wollersheim.com

Botham Vineyards
8180 Langberry Rd., Barneveld
(608) 924-1412
bothamvineyards.com

Toot + Kate's
109 S. Main St., Verona
(608) 497-1111
facebook.com/tootandkates

DELIGHT IN THE DÉCOR
AT ELLA'S DELI

Kids can be forgiven for not finishing their lunch at Ella's Deli and Ice Cream Parlor. There's so much going on at this kosher-style deli and ice cream parlor that even adults can have a hard time focusing on their food. Superheroes soar through the sky, the Beatles jam in a diorama, and a host of madcap characters entertain in tinker-y displays from floor to ceiling at this east side eatery that's been a must-see for families since 1976. Dig into a pastrami sandwich or bowl of matzo ball soup—or better yet, skip straight to the sundaes, malts, and splits from the 10-page dessert menu. On warm days, take a spin on the ornate 1920s carousel, an experience that's sure to be the cherry on top of a visit to this playful paradise.

2902 E. Washington Ave., (608) 241-5291
ellasdeli.com

GRAB A GREAT BURGER

Whether served with a pint and a Packers game or listed alongside elegant entrees, the burger is decidedly democratic in Madison. Bob's Bad Breath Burger at the Weary Traveler Freehouse tops organic Wisconsin beef with garlic, pickapeppa sauce, and goddess dressing, while the namesake burger at Graze combines ground short ribs, sirloin, and bacon (and rings in at $21). Choose among 14 creative burgers at Dotty Dumpling's Dowry or pair one of eight "posh" burgers at DLUX with a boozy shake. Try to coax the secret-sauce recipes for the Plazaburger and Gritty Burger from the staff at the Plaza Tavern and Nitty Gritty, respectively. Or let the Alchemy Café's bison burger or Harmony Bar & Grill's walnut burger prove that sometimes the best burgers bail on beef.

Weary Traveler Freehouse
1201 Williamson St., (608) 442-6207
wearytravelerfreehouse.com

Graze
1 S. Pinckney St., (608) 251-2700
grazemadison.com

Dotty Dumpling's Dowry
317 N. Frances St., (608) 259-0000
dottydumplingsdowry.com

DLUX
117 Martin Luther King Blvd., (608) 467-3130
dluxmadison.com

The Plaza Tavern
319 N. Henry St., (608) 255-6592
theplazatavern.com

Nitty Gritty
223 N. Frances St., (608) 251-2521
thegritty.com

Alchemy Café
1980 Atwood Ave., (608) 204-7644
alchemycafe.net

Harmony Bar & Grill
2201 Atwood Ave., (608) 249-4333
harmonybarandgrill.com

BECOME A CHEESEHEAD
AT FROMAGINATION

The past, present, and future of cheese come together tastefully at Fromagination. Ken Monteleone's charming Capitol Square shop is packed with fromage-focused food trays, gift baskets, and accessories. And lots of cheese. Cow's-, goat's- and sheep's-milk varieties mingle with cheddar, gouda, and small-batch specialties from Wisconsin, as well as varieties from France, Italy, England, and elsewhere. Here, an appreciation for the history of cheesemaking is matched only by enthusiasm for today's artisan cheesemakers putting new twists on traditions. Cheesemongers are happy to chat about cheese, slice a sample, make a sandwich, or pack a gourmet picnic. And Fromagination offers a cheese of the month program for those wishing to continue tasting and learning.

12 S. Carroll St., (608) 255-2430
fromagination.com

CHEERS TO WISCONSIN
WITH AN OLD FASHIONED

There are a few things you should know when ordering an old fashioned in Madison. First, the drink will be made with brandy—not whiskey—along with sugar, bitters, orange, and cherry. Second, you can get it "sweet" or "sour." And, finally, you may receive nods of approval by choosing the unofficial state cocktail. Every bar in the city knows how to make a proper Wisconsin-style old fashioned, but there's something special about sipping one at an old-school establishment. So if you find yourself at a supper club in need of a perfect complement to your fish fry dinner, or bellied up to a bar while a blizzard rages outside, order an old fashioned in the best Wisconsin tavern tradition.

INDULGE YOUR SWEET TOOTH
AT GAIL AMBROSIUS

There's chocolate, and then there is the culinary artistry of a chocolatier like Gail Ambrosius. The former cartographer launched her eponymous chocolate company in 2004, turning cacao sustainably grown half a world away into thousands of tiny, single-origin, gourmet truffles. The concoctions are intoxicating—cinnamon/cayenne, pistachio bomb, sweet curry with saffron, orange almond—but simpler flavors shine, too. Lucille's Vanilla, for instance, is reminiscent of chocolate pudding Ambrosius's mother used to make on the stovetop of their farm kitchen. Some flavors change seasonally; drool over the day's assortment at the cheerful Atwood Avenue shop.

2086 Atwood Ave., (608) 249-3500
gailambrosius.com

BITE INTO THE BRAT TRADITION

Whether at a big Badger tailgate or just chilling on your deck, a brat sizzling on the grill signals you're in Wisconsin. The bratwurst's popularity here goes all the way back to the 19th century, when immigrating Germans brought the sausage to the States. Today, the best way to cook a brat is fiercely debated—and often depends on where in Wisconsin you happen to be firing up the grill—but typically involves mustard, chopped onions, and sauerkraut as toppings and a bun sturdy enough to hold it all together. Wash it down with a locally brewed beer, and you have a truly Sconnie meal in your hands. You can swap recipes, or simply share enthusiasm, with thousands of fellow brat fans at the World's Largest Brat Fest, held each Memorial Day weekend.

TIP

Brats are sold at local grocery stores and are increasingly making their way onto Madison restaurant menus. For authentic, old-world bratwurst, check out Bavaria Sausage at 6317 Nesbitt Road, on the west side.

The World's Largest Brat Fest takes place over four days during Memorial Day weekend at the Alliant Energy Center.
bratfest.com

TAKE YOUR LICKS

Ice cream must be good in the Dairy State, right? You betcha! Babcock ice cream, which UW-Madison has been making at its dairy plant since the 1950s, is a tasty place to start. Enjoy a scoop at the Memorial Union or the Babcock Hall Dairy Store. And with four Madison locations, the Chocolate Shoppe ensures you're never far from a fix of mint avalanche or blue moon. But if you scream for ice cream, you'll go bonkers for frozen custard, a thicker, creamier frozen treat made with egg in addition to cream and sugar. Michael's Frozen Custard's three old-fashioned shops churn out perfectly concocted custard, while Culver's, the fast-food chain headquartered just outside of Madison, is spreading the joy of Wisconsin frozen custard across the country.

Babcock Hall Dairy Store
1605 Linden Dr., (608) 262-3045
babcockhalldairystore.wisc.edu

Daily Scoop at the Memorial Union
800 Langon St., (608) 265-3412
union.wisc.edu

Chocolate Shoppe
2302 Atwood Ave., (608) 204-2702
1726 Fordem Ave., (608) 241-2747
555 South Midvale Blvd., (608) 441-5248
46 State St., (608) 255-5454
chocolateshoppeicecream.com

Michael's Frozen Custard
2531 Monroe St., (608) 231-3500
5602 Schroeder Rd., (608) 276-8100
3826 Atwood Ave., (608) 222-4110
ilovemichaels.com

SAMPLE SOME SPIRITS

Happily, the eat-local movement extends to beverages. Old Sugar Distillery crafts brandy, whiskey, rum, ouzo, and honey liqueur and highlights each in special cocktails served at its popular downtown tasting room and patio. Yahara Bay Distillers produces more than 20 different small-batch spirits, from whiskey and gin to apple crisp liqueur and crancello made with Wisconsin cranberries. Death's Door Spirits makes white whisky, artisan peppermint schnapps, and other spirits utilizing crops from Washington Island, off the tip of Wisconsin's peninsula. Learn all about meads—a historic drink made from fermented water and honey—through samples at Bos Meadery. And don't miss the new Wollersheim Distillery out in Prairie du Sac, where you can taste apple brandy and other spirits.

Please confirm tour and tasting room availability before visiting any of these distilleries.

Old Sugar Distillery
931 E. Main St., (608) 260-0812
oldsugardistillery.com

Yahara Bay Distillers
3118 Kingsley Way, (608) 275-1050
yaharabay.com

Death's Door Spirits
2220 Eagle Dr., Middleton, (608) 831-1083
deathsdoorspirits.com

Bos Meadery
849 E. Washington Ave., (608) 628-3792
bosmeadery.com

Wollersheim Distillery
7876 WI-88, Prairie du Sac, (608) 643-6515
wollersheim.com

BRING HOME
TASTES OF MADISON

Made-here food items are great buys! Small-batch preserves and syrups from popular local food producer Quince & Apple range in flavors from peach chamomile to lime and cucumber. Potter's Crackers' organic artisan snacks come in such equally creative varieties as applewood smoked and caramelized onion. The 100 Mile Sauce Company makes barbecue sauce, ketchup, and more using local, sustainable ingredients, while Yumbutter seeks to save the world with its organic nut butters and buy-one, feed-one business model. Porchlight Products' jams, jellies, and pancake mixes are made by members of marginalized communities; Off the Block Salsa comes from the work of at-risk youth through the Mentoring Positives Program. Also buzzworthy? Mad Urban Bees' honey, harvested from city parks and gardens.

Quince & Apple
(608) 301-5433
quinceandapple.com

Potter's Crackers
(608) 663-5005
potterscrackers.com

100 Mile Sauce Company
(608) 535-9095
100milesauce.com

Yumbutter
yumbutter.com

Porchlight Products
(608) 257-2534
porchlightproducts.org

Off the Block Salsa
(608) 819-6200
mentoringpositives.org

Mad Urban Bees
(608) 622-7965
madurbanbees.com

DRINK IN A VIEW

The perfect accompaniment to a cocktail? A gorgeous view of the city! Perched atop the Madison Museum of Contemporary Art, the sleek Fresco restaurant boasts fantastic vistas year-round; in warm months, take a seat in the museum's outdoor sculpture garden and look out onto the bustle of State Street. At the nearby Brickhouse BBQ, grab a spot under lights strung above the rooftop deck and let the cool sights of the city offset the heat of your meal. And over on Langdon Street, the hip new Graduate Hotel's rooftop bar, the Madison Blind, offers fresh looks out at Lake Mendota and the Capitol.

Fresco
227 State St., (608) 663-7374
frescomadison.com

Brickhouse BBQ
408 W. Gorham St., (608) 257-7675
thebrickhousebbq.com

The Madison Blind
601 Langdon St., (608) 257-4391
graduatemadison.com

GET A TASTE OF MADISON
ON A FOOD TOUR

Take a walk, bike, or bus ride to sample, sip, and learn about Madison's amazing local food. Madison Eats Food Tours takes you to half a dozen local eateries, where you can meet the people cooking up all the deliciousness; Atwood Avenue, Williamson Street, and downtown are typical destinations. Madison Food Explorers can show you culinary highlights on the isthmus, or set your sights on Friday happy hour or Sunday brunch, with history, architecture, and other entertaining knowledge mixed in. Capital City Food Tours digs into the restaurants and stories of Middleton and the Capitol Square. Rather drink your way across town? Then join Hop Head Tours in visiting local breweries, wineries, and distilleries by bus or bike.

Madison Eats
madisoneats.net

Madison Food Explorers
madisonfoodexplorers.com

Capital City Food Tours
capitalcityfoodtours.com

Hop Head Tours
hopheadtours.com

DINE ALONG A LAKE

A lakeside view enhances any meal. Pair pastas and pizzas with sangria and a panorama of Lake Monona from the expansive deck or cozy dining room at Paisan's, or enjoy Sardine's happy hour oysters or weekend brunch on its patio overlooking the waters. Laid-back seafood spot Nau-ti-gal is tucked along the Yahara River where it meets Lake Mendota, and Christy's Landing brings a party to Lake Waubesa with food, drinks, music, and volleyball. At the Edgewater hotel, perched along the shoreline of Lake Mendota, the elegant Statehouse serves modern Midwestern fare, while its more casual counterpart, the Boathouse, is all about burgers and brats, served indoors or out. Want to dine on the water? Hop aboard one of the Betty Lou Cruises, which set sail on Lakes Mendota and Monona.

Paisan's
131 W. Wilson St., (608) 257-3832
paisansrestaurant.biz

Sardine
617 Williamson St., (608) 441-1600
sardinemadison.com

Nau-ti-gal
5360 Westport Rd., (608) 246-3130
nautigal.com

Christy's Landing
2952 Waubesa Ave., (608) 222-5391
christyslanding.com

The Edgewater
1001 Wisconsin Pl., (608) 535-8200
theedgewater.com

Betty Lou Cruises
(608) 246-3138
bettyloucruises.com

MUSIC AND ENTERTAINMENT

PAIR MUSIC WITH FOOD
AT CONCERTS ON THE SQUARE

On six glorious Wednesdays each summer, the State Capitol lawn becomes the place to gather, relax, dine, and listen to live music. The brainchild of a local philanthropist, the Concerts on the Square series has been a highlight of Madison summers since 1984. Each week, thousands of concertgoers set down blankets, open up picnic baskets and bottles of wine, and take in the sounds of the Wisconsin Chamber Orchestra. Performances mix classical music gems with pop hits, and it's exactly this combination of high-caliber and down-to-earth sensibilities that make this event such a delight. If you like what you hear, check out the WCO's indoor mainstage season that kicks off in the fall.

Concerts run late June to early August.
(608) 257-0638
wcoconcerts.org

SEE THE BIG SHOW
AT OVERTURE CENTER

Sure, it's a bit off Broadway, but Overture Center is your ticket to the hottest blockbuster musicals hitting the road. The downtown performing arts center brings in about seven touring Broadway productions each season, from classics like *Phantom of the Opera*, *Cabaret*, and *RENT* to newer, buzzier shows such as *Wicked*, *The Lion King*, and *The Book of Mormon*, ensuring there's always something great to see—or see again! Find your spot among Overture Hall's 2,000-plus seats, settle in, and let the fantastic music, dance, costumes, and undeniable razzle-dazzle of Broadway take you away.

201 State St., (608) 258-4141
overturecenter.org

HAVE AN ENHANCED CINEMATIC EXPERIENCE
AT SUNDANCE CINEMAS

When Sundance Cinemas opened in 2007 at the Hilldale Shopping Center, it offered an elegant alternative to the typical movie theater experience. Specializing in indie, art, foreign, and documentary films, the handsome six-screen cinema allows moviegoers to reserve their seats. And did they ever step up concessions! Sandwiches, pizza, smoothies, organic white popcorn with real butter, local beer, cocktails, and wine are a few of the refreshments you can take inside. Madison was the first city to receive a cinema from Robert Redford's Sundance Group. And while other theaters have since followed suit, expanding their menus beyond candy and soda and adding plusher seats, Sundance is still the place to go when you want to see a film, not a flick.

430 N. Midvale Blvd., (608) 316-6900
sundancecinemas.com

SPOT ANIMALS
AT COWS ON THE CONCOURSE

A herd of cows congregating downtown serves as the annual kick-off to June Dairy Month in Dane County, as well as a reminder of Wisconsin's legacy as "America's Dairyland." At Cows on the Concourse, a free, family-friendly event, visitors can meet—and even pet—cows and calves from local farms, take part in a scavenger hunt, learn about the dairy economy, and more. Need a snack? Enjoy a grilled cheese sandwich and—what else?—a bottle of cold milk.

Held on a Saturday in early June on the Capitol Square.
cowsontheconcourse.org

HEAR A JAZZ LEGEND

Among the many high notes of Madison's music scene are the world-renowned jazz musicians who call the city home. Wisconsin-born and UW-educated pianist Ben Sidran has played with Steve Miller, Boz Scaggs, and Diana Ross and now tours the globe. "Funky drummer" Clyde Stubblefield got his start with James Brown but has gigged with his eponymous band in Madison since the 1970s. And while Richard Davis recently retired from teaching jazz at UW, the legendary bassist—who's performed or recorded with the likes of Sarah Vaughan, Frank Sinatra, Miles Davis, Van Morrison, and Bruce Springsteen—continues to work on issues of social justice. Jazz fans should check out the Brink Lounge and Liliana's for the next generation of stars.

Brink Lounge
701 E. Washington Ave., (608) 661-8599
thebrinklounge.com

Liliana's
2951 Triverton Pike Dr., Fitchburg, (608) 442-4444
lilianasrestaurant.com

CELEBRATE
SCHOOL SPIRIT
AT THE VARSITY BAND CONCERT

You could go to the Kohl Center for a UW basketball or hockey game. But the best dose of Badger spirit may come when the players leave the arena and the venerable University of Wisconsin Marching Band holds court. The annual Varsity Band Concert is a spectacle in the best sense of the word, bringing together guest singers, surprise performers, pyrotechnics, and, of course, the high-energy band that plays pop hits and traditional tunes with equal fanfare. A highlight of the extravaganza is seeing band director Mike Leckrone fly over the crowd or engage in some other creatively crazy stunt.

Held three evenings in April.
601 W. Dayton St., (608) 265-4120
badgerband.com

GET YOUR TICKET
TO THE WISCONSIN FILM FESTIVAL

Many Madisonians eagerly await spring, but local film buffs have an extra reason to anticipate the change of seasons. The Wisconsin Film Festival takes place each April, screening roughly 150 cinematic works over eight days at six city venues for nearly 30,000 film fans. Considered the largest university-produced film fest in the nation, the event presents a diverse mix: independent and international films, documentaries and avant-garde works, restored classics and children's movies all draw eager crowds. A highlight is the focus on films with Wisconsin ties, whether through a piece's setting, theme, or creator. Bring on the popcorn!

Held each March.
wifilmfest.org

GROOVE TOGETHER
AT DANE DANCES

What if dancing could build bridges? What if listening to music together could create bonds? That's the simple, beautiful, and powerful idea behind Dane Dances. Launched in 2000, the outdoor concert series held every Friday evening in August provides a welcoming atmosphere and brings a diverse crowd together. Madisonians and visitors of all ages and backgrounds meet at the Monona Terrace rooftop, where local DJs and R&B, funk, salsa, and merengue bands create beats that get people up on their feet and out on the dance floor. A handful of area restaurants are represented while backdrops of Lake Monona and the Capitol help set the stage for upbeat and up-tempo nights.

Held every Friday in August.
(608) 719-8846
danedances.org

ROCK OUT!

The magic of live music finds a welcome home at local concert venues, grand as well as intimate. The Majestic, Barrymore, and Orpheum theaters, all built in the early 1900s and full of historic charm, are hotspots for rock, pop, and indie bands, while the smaller High Noon Saloon, Frequency, and Brink Lounge are popular for both local and out-of-town performers. Catch big-name touring acts when they light up the Alliant Energy Center, the Kohl Center, or Overture Center, the city's largest venues. And hear talented local musicians at bars, restaurants, and cafés like the Harmony Bar & Grill (for blues, rock, and more) and Crescendo Espresso Bar (for singer-songwriters).

Majestic Theatre
115 King St., (608) 255-0901
majesticmadison.com

Barrymore Theatre
2090 Atwood Ave., (608) 241-8864
barrymorelive.com

Orpheum Theater
216 State St., (608) 250-2600
madisonorpheum.com

High Noon Saloon
701 E. Washington Ave., (608) 268-1122
high-noon.com

The Frequency
121 E. Main St., (608) 819-8777
madisonfrequency.com

Brink Lounge
701 E. Washington Ave., (608) 661-8599
thebrinklounge.com

Alliant Energy Center
1919 Alliant Energy Center Way, (608) 267-3976
alliantenergycenter.com

Kohl Center
601 W. Dayton St., (608) 263-5645
uwbadgers.com

Overture Center
201 State St., (608) 258-4141
overturecenter.org

Harmony Bar & Grill
2201 Atwood Ave., (608) 249-4333
harmonybarandgrill.com

Crescendo Espresso Bar
1859 Monroe St., (608) 284-7908
crescendomadison.com

EXHIBITION-HOP
ON GALLERY NIGHT

How much art can you see in a single evening? That's the wonderful challenge of Gallery Night. Organized each spring and fall by the Madison Museum of Contemporary Art, the event is a chance to check out exhibitions across the city. Roughly 60 galleries, museums, studios, and other businesses—some that don't normally showcase art—open their doors and invite the public in to browse artwork, meet artists, and enjoy refreshments and live entertainment. It's a lively time to support favorite galleries and discover new art hubs.

Held one Friday each May and October.
(608) 257-0158
mmoca.org

DANCE THE WINTER AWAY
AT KID DISCO

When winter has the whole family feeling stir crazy, what do you do? You Kid Disco. This massively popular series at the Great Dane Pub & Brewing Co. encourages parents and kids alike to let loose. On select winter Saturdays from late morning to midafternoon at the Dane's Hilldale or Eastside brewery outposts, DJ Nick Nice, one of the city's top emcees, spins hits while kids and grownups alike boogie down amid bubbles flowing from a machine. Not the dancing type? No worries. Just take a seat, order a German pils or a hoppy IPA from this beloved local brewery, and watch the insane amount of all-ages fun taking place on the dance floor.

Great Dane Pub & Brewing Co.
357 Price Pl., (608) 661-9400
876 Jupiter Dr., (608) 442-1333
greatdanepub.com

CELEBRATE HERITAGE

All year long, events highlight Madison's diverse influences. The International Festival features performances by dozens of artists representing cultures from around the world. At the On Wisconsin Spring Powwow, the UW-Madison Native American student organization Wunk Sheek presents dancing and demonstrations. Syttende Mai showcases Stoughton's Norwegian heritage with everything from folk dances to traditional crafts to a parade, while a pasta dinner, bocce tournament, and live music are just a few of the components of Festa Italia. Juneteenth commemorates emancipation and honors African American history with a parade that leads to a family-friendly celebration, and Africa Fest focuses on the food, music, and art of the continent. And everyone is invited to ring in the Hmong New Year with guest speakers, food, games, and cultural programs.

The International Festival is in February
at Overture Center.
overturecenter.org

The On Wisconsin Spring Powwow
is held each April at the
Alliant Energy Center.

Syttende Mai runs over three days in May
throughout the town of Stoughton.
stoughtonwi.com/syttendemai/

Festa Italia takes place in early June at McKee
Farms Park in Fitchburg.
iwcmadison.com

Juneteenth is held one Saturday
in June at Penn Park.
kujimcsd.org

Africa Fest runs in August at Central Park.
africanassociationofmadison.org

The Hmong New Year Celebration takes
place the last weekend of November
at the Alliant Energy Center.
hmongmadison.com

FEEL THE BREESE

It's an unconfirmed scientific fact that music sounds better outside, and Breese Stevens Field might be the best evidence for the case. The city-owned historic athletic stadium, which was built in 1926 and now holds a spot on the National Registry of Historic Places, is the home turf of several sports teams and a regular site of special events. But its newest claim to fame is serving as the coolest venue for outdoor concerts. The Avett Brothers, the Steve Miller Band, Wilco, and Cake have all rocked out at the park, which feels perfectly at home on the rapidly rejuvenating East Washington Avenue corridor.

917 E. Mifflin St., (608) 622-1414
breesestevensfield.com

GO HOG WILD
AT THE DANE COUNTY FAIR

Agriculture meets entertainment at the Dane County Fair, an event that dates back to 1851. From a tractor parade, pig races, and stunt shows to a carnival and live music, all sorts of family-friendly entertainment comes together for five days at the Alliant Energy Center. There are also dog demos, agricultural exhibitions, farm-animal judging, and a kiddie farm where you can meet baby animals. And don't forget the food! Fair fare includes corn dogs, cotton candy, funnel cakes, root beer floats, cheese curds, and cream puffs, plus all sorts of edibles on a stick—pork chops, cheesecake, and much more.

Held each July at the Alliant Energy Center.
danecountyfair.com

FEST WITH THE BEST

Madison has perfected the art of the summer festival, and nearly every weekend brings a new combination of live music, local food, and friendly vibes. The Marquette Waterfront Festival begins with the Fool's Flotilla of canoes, kayaks, and more paddling from Lake Menota to Yahara Place Park. Next comes the Isthmus Jazz Festival, which celebrates the genre at the Memorial Union Terrace, followed by La Fête de Marquette highlighting music from the French-speaking world at Central Park. AtwoodFest marches to the funky beat of its beloved near-east-side neighborhood, while the Sugar Maple Traditional Music Festival mixes bluegrass, country, and more at Lake Farm County Park. The five-decades-strong Orton Park Festival boasts an eclectic lineup at its namesake park. And the Madison World Music Festival brings global sounds to both the Terrace and the wonderfully weird Willy Street Fair.

The Marquette Waterfront Festival is held in early to mid-June.
marquette-neighborhood.org

The Isthmus Jazz Festival takes place in mid-June.
isthmus.com

La Fête de Marquette is held in mid-July.
wil-mar.org

AtwoodFest happens in late July.
atwoodfest.com

The Sugar Maple Traditional Music Festival runs in early August.
sugarmaplefest.org

The Orton Park Festival takes place in late August.
marquette-neighborhood.org

The Madison World Music Festival and Willy Street Fair are held in mid-September.
union.wisc.edu, cwd.org

GEEK OUT
AT TRIVIA NIGHT

Madisonians are an intelligent lot, and they put their knowledge to fun use at local trivia nights. Plenty of pubs offer these brain-teasing competitions—in which teams answer questions on everything from sports stats to pop-culture happenings—with atmospheres ranging from casual to cutthroat. The High Noon Saloon also hosts spirited meetings of the minds: the concert venue teams up with Strictly Discs for Music Trivia to test players' music knowledge, while Nerd Nite brings together drinks, presentations, and "nerdery of all sorts." And Pundamonium sees 10 contestants battling it out to see who can come up with the best puns based on prompts until the last two compete in a final pun-off.

Find a list of local trivia nights at leaguetrivia.com.

High Noon Saloon
701 E. Washington Ave., (608) 268-1122
high-noon.com

PARTY IN THE STREET
AT LIVE ON KING STREET

When the century-old Majestic Theatre reopened in 2007, it brought fresh energy to King Street. And when the theater launched Live on King Street just out its front doors in 2011, it made the short street just off the Capitol Square even cooler. The popular-from-the-start outdoor concert series sets a stage in front of the theater and thousands of music lovers fill the street to hear acts like Ra Ra Riot, Horseshoes & Hand Grenades, Cloud Cult, Ziggy Marley, and The Head and the Heart play. It all feels hip and positive, natural and effortless, as if these concerts have been a part of the Madison live-music landscape forever.

Live on King Street concerts take place on select Fridays
from June to September.

115 King St., (608) 255-0901
majesticmadison.com

CATCH AN AL FRESCO FLICK

Make the most of summer by watching a film outdoors. Lay a blanket where the Badgers play and take in a family-friendly flick on the north-end video board at the annual Movie Night at Camp Randall Stadium. Breese Stevens Field's Catch & Reel series pairs a Friday night fish fry with a movie screening once a month throughout the summer, while Movies on the Water at the Edgewater offers a popular film every Tuesday at sunset from the lakefront hotel's plaza. The Terrace After Dark series at the Memorial Union offers both Lakeside Cinema with themed movie screenings on Mondays at sundown and the new Lakeside Family Films on select Sunday nights. And in the Madison Museum of Contemporary Art's sculpture garden, watch an avant-garde film at Rooftop Cinema.

Movie Night at Camp Randall takes place in June.
1440 Monroe St., (608) 262-1866
uwbadgers.com

**Catch & Reel is held once a month
in June, July, and August.**
917 E. Mifflin St., (608) 622-1414
breesestevensfield.com

**Movies on the Water takes place Tuesdays
from June through September.**
1001 Wisconsin Pl., (608) 535-8189
theedgewater.com

**Lakeside Cinema takes place Mondays from late
May to early September; Lakeside Family Films is
on select Sundays June through August.**
800 Langdon St., (608) 265-3000
union.wisc.edu

**Rooftop Cinema is held on select nights
in June and August.**
227 State St., (608) 257-0158
mmoca.org

TUNE IN TO ECLECTIC CONCERT SERIES

The only thing better than a great musical performance is knowing that there's more to come. Each summer, Central Park Sessions hosts themed concerts—honky tonk, Irish, Saharan, and other globally inspired "sessions"—in the popular near-east-side Central Park, and Lunchtime Live brings some of the Madison area's most beloved bands to the Capitol Square for midday performances. Jazz lovers should check out Jazz at Five, which showcases a wide range of top-notch performers at the top of State Street, and the Tandem Press Friday Jazz Series, which sees the innovative, UW-affiliated printmaking studio welcoming artists from the university's Jazz Studies Program. And mark your calendars for Make Music Madison, which kicks off summer with a citywide day of free outdoor music.

Central Park Sessions take place on select
Thursday and Friday evenings July through
September at Central Park.
202 S. Ingersol St.
facebook.com/cpsessions/

Lunchtime Live runs Tuesdays from July through
September on the Capitol Square.
visitdowntownmadison.com

Jazz at Five is held Wednesday evenings in August
where State Street meets the Capitol Square.
jazzatfive.org

The Tandem Press Friday Jazz Series occurs
on select evenings in the fall and spring.
1743 Commercial Ave.
tandempress.wisc.edu

Make Music Madison takes place on the
summer solstice each June.
makemusicmadison.org

TAKE TO THE TERRACE

It may be the official outdoor hangout for UW-Madison students, but the Memorial Union Terrace has long been the preferred gathering spot for anyone who wants to chill by the lake. Grab a sunburst-shaped metal chair—the eye-catching orange, yellow, and green seats are Madison icons in their own right—and make the difficult choice between a sizzling brat, a scoop of Babcock ice cream, or one of 30 beers on tap, many of them made in Wisconsin. Or make the decision a lot easier and go for all three. By day, soak up the sunshine and watch boats bob out on Lake Mendota; at night, enjoy a festive atmosphere and live music on Thursdays, Fridays, and Saturdays in the summer.

800 Langdon St., (608) 265-3000
union.wisc.edu

Photo Credit: Katie Vaughn

SPORTS AND RECREATION

CHEER ON THE BADGERS
AT CAMP RANDALL

Perhaps more important than who wins or loses (but still, go Badgers!) are the traditions that have made Madison one of the best college football towns in the country. Football Saturdays are daylong celebrations that begin with donning your red and white best and heading out to tailgate. Enjoy a brat and a beer with fellow fans on Regent Street before entering the historic Camp Randall Stadium, built in 1917 on the grounds of a camp where Civil War troops trained. Then watch everything from Bucky doing push-ups each time the Badgers score to many of the 80,000 spectators getting up to "Jump Around" to students and alumni alike singing the time-honored "Varsity." Stick around for the Fifth Quarter, when the UW Marching Band takes to the field for a post-game show.

1440 Monroe St., (608) 262-1866
uwbadgers.com

STOP AND SMELL THE ROSES
AT OLBRICH BOTANICAL GARDENS

From an expansive rose garden to a traditional English garden to perennial, wildflower, meadow, rock, and herb gardens, there's a lot to explore at Olbrich Botanical Gardens. Be sure to meander over to the Thai Garden, complete with sculptures (kids love greeting the stone elephants), reflecting pools, and the only Thai pavilion in the continental United States. The Bolz Conservatory makes Olbrich a must-visit in the winter, too. It's always hot and humid inside the glass pyramid-shaped greenhouse, which keeps the more than 750 tropical plants as happy as the visitors who come in for a dose of warmth. Plant sales, concerts, and special events are held year-round; don't miss *GLEAM*, an illuminated art exhibition held in the fall, and Blooming Butterflies, which sends butterflies fluttering in the conservatory each summer.

3330 Atwood Ave., (608) 264-4550
olbrich.org

VISIT AN ANIMAL KINGDOM
AT THE HENRY VILAS ZOO

For more than a century, the Henry Vilas Zoo has brought wildlife of the world to Madison. The 28-acre public zoo is one of just a handful in the country that are free to visit—and it's been that way since it opened in 1911! Say hello to a lion, peek at penguins, flamingos, and lemurs, and watch orangutans play. Pop into the Tropical Rainforest Aviary to see colorful birds, or the Herpetarium to glimpse snakes, a tortoise, and fish. A highlight is the new Arctic Passage, complete with energetic polar bears and grizzly bears, and kids won't want to leave without taking a spin on the electric train or Conservation Carousel, featuring zoo animals in place of the typical horses.

702 S. Randall Ave., (608) 258-9490
vilaszoo.org

FEEL THE THRILL OF THE HILL
AT ELVER PARK

There's a strong possibility that nothing makes you feel more like a kid again than zipping down a snowy hill. So grab a sled, saucer, toboggan, or tube and put that hypothesis to the test at Elver Park. This west-side park boasts a playground, sports courts, a skating rink, and trails. But after a blizzard, the nearly 500-foot-hill is where you'll set your sights. Hoist yourself up to the top, teeter your sled over the edge, and—*whoosh!*—sail down over the slope. Chances are, you'll land in a pile of snow, mittens, and laughter … and jump up to do it all over again.

1250 McKenna Blvd., (608) 266-4711
cityofmadison.com/parks

BE AN IRON-FAN
AT IRONMAN WISCONSIN

It's the most intense triathlon math: A 2.4-mile swim in Lake Monona plus a 112-mile bike through the hilly farmland of Dane County plus a full 26.2-mile marathon through the streets of downtown Madison add up to Ironman Wisconsin. If you think the spectacle of nearly 3,000 swimmers thrashing through the lake at 7 a.m. is something, stick around until nighttime, when competitors cross the finish line in front of the illuminated Capitol. Ironman Wisconsin is known as a difficult course, but its reputation for enthusiastic spectator support the entire day is even stronger.

Held the second Sunday of September.
ironman.com/wisconsin

LINGER IN THE LANDSCAPE
AT THE ARBORETUM

A 1,200-acre oasis on the near-west side, the UW-Madison Arboretum is an ecological wonderland. Prairies, savannas, forests, and wetlands coexist here, the birthplace of ecological restoration. Hundreds of native plants showcase the unique beauty of the southern Wisconsin landscape, while special gardens let you view additional species of plants and flowers. Visitors can explore the Arb via 20-plus miles of footpaths and boardwalks, and each season brings new reasons to hike. Find information and nature-themed art at the Visitor Center, or take your pick among interesting and educational walks (held day and night), workshops, and events offered throughout the year.

1207 Seminole Hwy., (608) 263-7888
arboretum.wisc.edu

SCORE A HOME RUN OF FUN
AT A MALLARDS GAME

Take you out to the ballgame? Sure thing, but you'll want to bring your family or a pack of friends when you're off to see the Mallards. Part of the Northwoods summer collegiate baseball league, the team hosts games positively packed with entertainment— from Maynard the Duck zooming in on a zip line to games and giveaways in between innings, with some pretty high-quality baseball squeezed in, too. Warner Park, better known as the Duck Pond, is incredibly family friendly, and at its all-inclusive Duck Blind party deck, when the brats are hot and the Great Dane beer is cold, no one will judge you if you forget about the old ball game.

The season runs from late May through August.
2920 N. Sherman Ave., (608) 246-4277
mallardsbaseball.com

TAKE A HIKE
ON THE ICE AGE TRAIL

The Ice Age National Scenic Trail makes a thousand-mile zigzag through Wisconsin, traversing through 31 different counties and connecting hikers with the diverse beauty of the state. A portion of the trail—which is one of eight National Scenic Trails in the country—runs just west of Madison. Jump on at the Ice Age Junction on McKee Road and head south on the Verona Segment; a 2.4-mile hike takes you past neighborhoods and soccer fields and into pretty prairies. Or if you want a little more scenic drama, take the Ice Age Trail Alliance's recommendation and check out the 2.5-mile Table Bluff segment north of Cross Plains, known for its ridgetop views.

Ice Age Junction
7578 McKee Rd.
iceagetrail.org

CELEBRATE AUTUMN
AT AN ORCHARD

Come to an area orchard to pluck some apples or a pick out a pumpkin; stay for the smorgasbord of autumnal activities offered. Eugster's is the grandaddy, boasting wagon rides, corn mazes, a petting farm, fall festival entertainment, and plenty of goodies like caramel apples and fresh-baked pies in its bakery. Sutter's Ridge is a fall playground, with tractors to pedal, hay bales to climb, kittens to cuddle, and warm apple cider doughnuts to devour, while hayrides and live bluegrass music are just some of the fun at the Norwegian-style Eplegaarden. Appleberry Farm is smaller, but big on charm, with hayrides, farm tours, and special apple cider brats. For a nighttime treat, consider Door Creek Orchard's exclusive Heirloom Apple Dinner at its sustainable apple farm.

Eugster's Farm Market
3865 WI-138, Stoughton, (608) 873-3822
eugsters.com

Sutter's Ridge Family Farm
2074 Sutter Dr., Mt. Horeb, (608) 832-6445
suttersridge.com

Eplegaarden
2227 Fitchburg Rd., Fitchburg, (608) 845-5966
eplegaarden.com

Appleberry Farm
8079 Maurer Rd., Cross Plains, (608) 798-2780
theappleberryfarm.com

Door Creek Orchard
3252 Vilas Rd., Cottage Grove, (608) 838-4762
doorcreekorchard.com

SEE WHERE EAGLES SOAR
IN SAUK PRAIRIE

It's always thrilling to spot a bald eagle in nature, and you're almost certain to do so come winter in Sauk City and Prairie du Sac. From December through February, the small towns northwest of Madison, known collectively as Sauk Prairie, attract eagles due to a dam that prevents a portion of the Wisconsin River from freezing. Morning is the best time to watch the birds, which arrive in dozens each year to fish and perch on riverside trees. Glimpse them from the Ferry Bluff Eagle Council Outlook (with spotting scopes available for use), from your car at the Prairie du Sac Hydroelecric Dam, or during Sauk Prairie Bald Eagle Watching Days, two days that combine eagle watching with presentations, kids' activities, and a pancake breakfast.

Sauk Prairie Bald Eagle Watching Days are held in January.
eaglewatchingdays.org

TIP
Always keep at least 100 yards between you and an eagle for safety.

CYCLE THE CITY
ON THE CAPITAL CITY STATE TRAIL

A greatest-hits bike tour of Madison, the Capital City State Trail takes you through downtown and out into marshlands, all along an easy 17-mile paved path. Starting on the southwest end, pass fields and forests until you reach Olin Park. From here, soak up Madison's stunning skyline as you ride between John Nolen Drive and Lake Monona. Cruise past Monona Terrace on your way to the funky Schenk-Atwood neighborhood and finally arrive at Olbrich Botanical Gardens. Wanna keep riding? Near the northeast end of the trail, you can pick up the 52-mile Glacial Drumlin State Trail. Or back near your starting point, connect with the 40-mile Military Ridge State Trail. If you need a set of wheels, rent a bright red B-Cycle; stations are set up all over the city.

Wisconsin Department of Natural Resources
(888) 936-7463
dnr.wi.gov/topic/parks/name/capcity/

B-Cycle
(800) 473-4742
madison.bcycle.com

TIP
A state trail pass is required for bicyclists ages 16 and above who ride on the nine miles of the Capital City State Trail that run through the Capital Springs E-way south of Madison.

PLAY
AT TENNEY PARK

While the city of Madison maintains more than 230 public greenspaces, a standout is Tenney Park on the near-east side. Back in 1899, local attorney Daniel K. Tenney donated 14 acres of marshland—the spot where Lake Mendota meets the Yahara River—on the condition that it become a park. This and other donations big and small led to a flourishing of park-building across the city from the 1890s through the 1930s. Today, Tenney Park accommodates a wide range of activities, from fishing to ice skating to soccer, volleyball, and softball. Yet it never loses its peaceful atmosphere. It remains a preferred place year-round for picnicking, bird-watching, and taking long walks and jogs along winding paths and over graceful bridges.

1414 E. Johnson St., (608) 266-4711
cityofmadison.com/parks

FEEL THE FLOWER POWER
AT POPE FARM CONSERVANCY

Imagine one of Wisconsin's rolling fields devoted to sunflowers instead of corn. That wish comes true each summer at Pope Farm Conservancy. The 105-acre nature preserve owned by the Town of Middleton offers eight miles of walking trails, tables, and grassy expanses for picnicking, and beautiful views of Lake Mendota and Madison year-round. But during Sunflower Days at the peak of summer, the dazzling draw is the roughly 500,000 sunflowers standing tall in full glorious yellow bloom. Locals are known to drop everything when they hear that the flowers are showing, flocking to the field from sunrise to sunset, knowing all too well that the magic is fleeting.

Flowers bloom in late July or early August.
7440 W. Old Sauk Rd., Verona
popefarmconservancy.org

RUN LIKE MAD
AT CRAZYLEGS

In a city chock full of races, it's hard for one to stand out—but the Crazylegs Classic certainly does. The 8K run kicks off near the Capitol, winds its way through the UW-Madison campus along Observatory Drive and out to Picnic Point, where it ends dramatically on the 50-yard line of Camp Randall Stadium. (A two-mile walk shares the start and end points.) The race, named for former football player and athletic director Elroy "Crazylegs" Hirsch, began in 1982 and has attracted up to about 20,000 participants each year, despite Wisconsin's unpredictable spring weather. The beer served at the post-race party doesn't hurt.

Held each April.
(608) 261-5347
crazylegsclassic.com

TAKE TO THE LAKE

You don't need to own a boat to get out on Madison's famous lakes. Dip a toe into paddlesports on peaceful Lake Wingra by renting a canoe, kayak, or rowboat from Wingra Boats. You can also give stand-up paddleboarding a try, or opt for one of the outfitter's utterly Instagrammable white, swan-shaped paddleboats. Brittingham Boats provides access to Lake Monona and Monona Bay, with a fleet of canoes, kayaks, and rowboats. Check out their stand-up paddleboard polo matches, as well as fun nighttime paddling events. Over at the Memorial Union on Lake Mendota, the Wisconsin Union rents out kayaks, canoes, and stand-up paddleboards, while Hoofers, the long-running UW student organization, offers lessons in sailing, windsurfing, and more by enthusiastic members.

Wingra Boats
824 Knickerbocker St., (608) 233-5332
wingraboats.com

Brittingham Boats
701 W. Brittingham Pl., (608) 250-2555
brittinghamboats.com

Wisconsin Union and Hoofers
800 Langdon St., (608) 262-1630
union.wisc.edu

BE GAME
FOR AN ALTERNATIVE SPORT

There's something for everyone to play or watch in Madison. Cheer on professional ultimate team the Madison Radicals, or get in on the fun by joining a league; the Madison Ultimate Frisbee Association organizes more than 3,500 players and 170 teams in the summer. The Mad Rollin' Dolls all-female, amateur roller derby league brings fast skating, hard hits, and empowerment to the track, while the Madison Gay Hockey Association combines athleticism and inclusion on the ice. The Mad City Ski team puts on entertaining shows all summer long, and Madison Log Rolling turns 19th-century lumberjack skills into modern-day competition, with rollers using fancy footwork to spin a log—and hopefully send their opponent splashing into the water.

Madison Log Rolling holds classes and competitions June through August at Lake Wingra.
madisonlogrolling.com

The Madison Radicals season runs April to August, with home games at Breese Stevens Field.
radicalsultimate.com

The Mad Rollin' Dolls hold home bouts at the Alliant Energy Center.
madrollindolls.com

Madison Gay Hockey Association competitions run from October to March.
madisongayhockey.org

The Mad City Ski Team performs most Sundays from Memorial Day weekend to Labor Day weekend at Law Park.
madcityskiteam.com

The Madison Ultimate Frisbee Association organizes leagues all year long.
mufa.org

HAVE A DOGGONE GOOD TIME
AT PRAIRIE MORAINE COUNTY PARK

In addition to 27 recreational parks, 15 wildlife areas, 29 natural resource areas, and two county forests, Dane County Parks maintains seven dog parks, and the unofficial favorite is at Prairie Moraine County Park. Dogs and humans alike enjoy wandering over hills and through woods and grassy meadows year-round in this expansive park located on the southeastern edge of Verona. Pups relish the chance to romp off leash, and their owners appreciate the park's beauty, cleanliness, and well-placed benches, as well as the friendliness of its visitors, whether the two- or four-foot variety.

6679 Wesner Rd., Verona, (608) 224-3730
parks-lwrd.countyofdane.com/park/PrairieMoraine

TIP
Dogs are welcome in all county parks with the purchase of a daily or annual permit, which can be purchased at the parks or at reservedane.com, plus a current municipal dog license.

FALL IN LOVE
WITH PICNIC POINT

You know that strip of land you see jutting out into Lake Mendota as you lounge at the Memorial Union Terrace? That's Picnic Point, and hiking out to its tip is an equally quintessential Madison experience. It's a roughly five-mile jaunt—along the tree-lined, shoreline-hugging Lakeshore Path—from the Terrace to Picnic Point. Or you can park at the base of university-owned Picnic Point and walk the nearly mile-long trail, passing beaches, fire circles, and Native American burial mounds, out to the end, where you're rewarded with panoramic views. The peninsula is popular for, yes, picnicking, as well as romance: it's a popular site for marriage proposals, and in 1992, the *San Francisco Examiner* ranked it one of the 10 best places in the world to kiss.

2002 University Bay Dr., (608) 262-2511
lakeshorepreserve.wisc.edu/visit/picnicpoint.htm

PLAY A ROUND
OF DISC GOLF

The coolest way to hit the links may be by ditching the clubs and ball. Disc golf, in which you toss a flying disc into a raised metal basket, has taken off in the Madison area. Like traditional golf, the goal is to hit the mark in the fewest strokes possible, and games take place on scenic courses—the most popular spots being Hiestand Park, Elver Park, Token Creek County Park, and the Capital Springs Recreation Area farther afield in Dane County. And like playing Frisbee, it's a heck of a lot of fun. Word of Madison's disc golf scene is getting out: The city was the site of the Professional Disc Golf Association Amateur World Championships in 2016.

Hiestand Park
4302 Milwaukee St.
cityofmadison.com/parks/discgolf

Elver Park
1250 McKenna Blvd.
cityofmadison.com/parks/discgolf

Token Creek County Park
6200 US-151, DeForest
parks-lwrd.countyofdane.com

Capital Springs Recreation Area
3101 Lake Farm Rd.
parks-lwrd.countyofdane.com

HAVE SOME FROSTY FUN
AT THE MADISON WINTER FESTIVAL

Whether you love snow or only wish you were the type who embraced the cold, the Madison Winter Festival will warm you up to the season. Each year, this outdoor event transforms the Capitol Square into a winter wonderland, with the help of some 90 truckloads of snow and the more than 20,000 spectators and athletes who come to play and compete. A cross-country ski race course loops around the Capitol, and family-friendly events like ice sculpting, sledding, snowshoeing, snowboarding, hockey, and curling showcase the possibilities of snow. Want to race? You can do so in sneakers or snowshoes, or on skis or a fat bike, and kids and dogs can get in on the fun, too.

Held over one weekend in February.
winter-fest.com

TAKE OVER THE ROADS
AT RIDE THE DRIVE

Madison is known for its bike-friendliness, and an annual event shows extra love for the two-wheeled set. Each summer, cars find alternative routes and give right of way to bicyclists who want to cruise Madison's main drags. John Nolen Drive, East Washington Avenue, Main Street, State Street, and other downtown roads all contribute to the five-mile loop that's open to bikers, bladers, skaters, and strollers. And cruising is just part of the action. Live music, food, merchandise tents, and kids' activities at special "villages" beckon bikers to hop off for a bit and extend the joy ride.

Typically held one day in the summer.
cityofmadison.com/parks/ridethedrive

HAVE A BALL
AT VITENSE GOLFLAND

It used to be that a trip to Vitense for a round of mini golf made a kid's day during summer vacation. But a major remodel a few years back expanded the fun to include all seasons and appeal to adults, too. The two classic outdoor miniature golf courses are still a warm-weather must—putt under a giant purple hippo or through a spinning waterwheel—or check out the new indoor course featuring a mini Madison, complete with a replica Capitol. The lighted par-three, nine-hole course makes for a fun summer evening for grown-up golfers, while the range is open year-round (and even boasts heated stalls in the winter). Batting cages, trampoline basketball, and a rock-climbing wall round out the all-ages activities.

5501 Schroeder Rd., (608) 271-1411
vitense.com

CULTURE AND HISTORY

FIND THE POLITICAL CENTER
AT THE WISCONSIN STATE CAPITOL

The literal centerpiece of the city, the Wisconsin State Capitol is home to both chambers of the state legislature, the Wisconsin Supreme Court, and the Office of the Governor. The white granite building was completed in 1917, featuring a dome topped with a gilded bronze statue making it the tallest structure in the city at 284 feet. The interior is carried out in marble and granite, made unique by the marks of several naturally occurring fossils. When you enter the grand rotunda, look up. The ceiling artwork, titled *Resources of Wisconsin,* features a female figure wrapped in the American flag as an embodiment of the state. Explore on your own or join one of several tours offered daily. During the summer, pop up to the sixth-floor observation deck for stellar views of downtown.

2 E. Main St., (608) 266-0382
tours.wisconsin.gov

ENJOY AL FRESCO ARIAS
AT OPERA IN THE PARK

You might not think to pair a picnic with an opera performance, but the two come together beautifully in Opera in the Park. Held for the past 15 years by Madison Opera, the event brings about 16,000 visitors to hilly Garner Park on the city's west side, where they dine and drink before the sun sets and the lights go up onstage. Then the company's stars, guest performers, the Madison Opera Chorus, and the Madison Symphony Orchestra begin the mid-summer magic, offering musical sneak peeks into the opera company's upcoming season, with some Broadway tunes and lighter fare mixed in for fun. While music fills the air, so do glow sticks held by audience members "conducting" from the grass.

Held each July at Garner Park.
(608) 238-8085
madisonopera.org

MAKE THE CAMPUS CLIMB
UP BASCOM HILL

As much a symbol of UW-Madison as Bucky Badger, Bascom Hill is the heart of the campus. The 850-foot-long drumlin rises 86 feet from its bottom on Park Street to its top, where the administration building Bascom Hall sits, but that 10 percent slope surely feels steeper to students lugging textbooks and laptops up its two concrete paths. Each fall, plastic pink flamingos dot the grassy space, a legendary 1979 prank that's now become a campus tradition and fundraiser. In winter, the hill becomes the site of epic snowball fights. And come spring, students relax—and sometimes even study—on the lawn and then pose for graduation photos with the larger-than-life statue of Abraham Lincoln that's been a part of the hill since 1909.

BE AMAZED BY THE ARTS
AT OVERTURE CENTER AND MMOCA

Madison's most venerable arts institutions come together at Overture Center for the Arts. The grand Cesar Pelli-designed arts hub opened in 2004 with two main theaters, several smaller performance spaces, and visual arts galleries and now counts the Madison Symphony Orchestra, Madison Opera, the Wisconsin Chamber Orchestra, Madison Ballet, Forward Theater Company, Kanopy Dance Company, Li Chiao-Ping Dance, Children's Theater of Madison, the Bach Dancing & Dynamite Society, and the James Watrous Gallery as resident companies. Overture also brings in touring acts and presents a bevy of free community events, including the Kids in the Rotunda entertainment series. Don't miss the adjacent Madison Museum of Contemporary Art, a dazzling 50,000-square-foot building that exhibits modern and contemporary art.

Overture Center
201 State St., (608) 258-4141
overturecenter.org

Madison Museum of Contemporary Art
225 State St., (608) 257-0158
mmoca.org

GET ON THE WRIGHT TRACK

Frank Lloyd Wright was born in southwestern Wisconsin, and the world-famous architect's signature Prairie style—with strong horizontal lines inspired by the Midwestern landscape—is reflected throughout the region. The Unitarian Meeting House, which he designed in the 1940s, is a mix of limestone, oak, and a dramatic copper roof and is home to the First Unitarian Society. While it's hard to imagine the city skyline without its centerpiece of Monona Terrace, Wright never got to see the now-iconic building. He proposed the lakeside convention center in 1938, but it wasn't built until 1997! And it's more than worth a day trip to Spring Green to see Taliesin, Wright's home, studio, and farm that was built in 1911 and continues the legacy of this visionary designer.

Unitarian Meeting House
900 University Bay Dr., (608) 233-9774
fusmadison.org

Monona Terrace
1 John Nolen Dr., (608) 261-4000
mononaterrace.com

Taliesin
5481 County Rd. C, Spring Green, (609) 588-7900
taliesinpreservation.org

FIND PATHS
TO ENLIGHTENMENT

Just south of Madison, the serene Deer Park Buddhist Center is a monastic and teaching center dedicated to making the teachings of the Buddha accessible. Visitors are welcome to tour two temples and see the Kalachakra Stupa, a shrine symbolizing the Buddha's enlightenment. Geshe Sopa, who founded Deer Park in 1976, taught Buddhist philosophy, language, and culture at UW-Madison for three decades. He has a relationship with the Dalai Lama, who has visited five times and holds an honorary degree from the university. Two nearby sites are also focused on the Dharmic religions: The Cambodian Buddhist Society, with a striking front gate and temple, offers resources on Cambodian Buddhist culture and the American Hindu Association Shiva Vishnu Temple is a Hindu temple and cultural center.

Deer Park Buddhist Center
4548 Schneider Dr., Oregon, (608) 835-5572
deerparkcenter.org

Cambodian Buddhist Society
Co. Rd. MM, Oregon, (608) 835-8136
facebook.com/pg/cambodianbuddhistsociety

Shiva Vishnu Temple
2138 S. Fish Hatchery Rd., Fitchburg, (608) 234-8634
aha-svtemple.org

DELVE INTO DANCE

Madison boasts a dance scene many bigger cities only dream of having. Madison Ballet has been a cultural cornerstone for decades, but it's hardly stuck in the past. The company puts an athletic spin on *The Nutcracker* each winter and offsets the classics with edgier fare, like its steampunk rock ballet *Dracula*. Kanopy Dance mingles guest choreographers with in-house talent, offering eclectic modern dance performances that are always high in quality. Li Chiao-Ping Dance explores themes of history, race, the body, and acceptance through emotionally charged, athletic, and thought-provoking contemporary dance. And Overture Center and the Wisconsin Union Theater regularly bring nationally acclaimed touring dance troupes to the stage.

Madison Ballet
(608) 278-7990
madisonballet.org

Kanopy Dance
(608) 255-2211
kanopydance.org

Li Chiao-Ping Dance
(608) 835-6590
lichiaopingdance.org

Overture Center for the Arts
(608) 258-4141
overturecenter.org

Wisconsin Union Theater
(608) 265-2787
uniontheater.wisc.edu

BOOK IT
TO THE MADISON PUBLIC LIBRARY

Books represent just one of many exciting discoveries to be made at the Madison Public Library. The eye-catching Central Library, which re-opened in 2013 after a $30 million renovation on the site of the original 1965 building, represents a new chapter in the look, feel, and purpose of libraries. In addition to books, the sleek and modern 120,000-square-foot space features lots of inviting spots to plop down with a read or a laptop, its own café, and a huge, bright children's area. And the library's innovative Bubbler program is responsible for creative hands-on workshops, cool after-hours events, an artist-in-residence program, and an incredibly interesting, inclusive, and ever-changing showcase of art.

201 W. Mifflin St., (608) 266-6300
madisonpubliclibrary.org

GLIMPSE SACRED EFFIGY MOUNDS

Native Americans built effigy mounds for hundreds of years, long before the "Four Lakes" area became known as Madison. Roughly 1,300 of the low earthen mounds—built in a range of sizes and forms, including animal shapes—have been identified here, making UW-Madison home to more of the sacred structures than any other university in the country. Built between 800 BC and 1200 AD, often on elevated land overlooking water, the mounds are believed to have been burial places as well as ceremonial sites, and those that remain are now protected by law. A bird effigy on the northern shore of Lake Mendota has a wingspan of more than 600 feet, while additional mounds can be seen on the top of Observatory Hill, near the tip of Picnic Point, and on the grounds of the Arboretum at UW.

The Wisconsin Department of Tourism maintains a list of effigy mounds on travelwisconsin.com.

LEARN A LOT
ON A MUSEUM-HOP

From history to science and beyond, there's plenty to explore at Madison museums. The state's native inhabitants, lumber industry, and progressive political legacy come alive at the Wisconsin Historical Museum, while the Wisconsin Veterans Museum uses exhibits and events to highlight the men and women of the state who have served in conflicts from the Civil War to today. The Harlem Renaissance Museum, meanwhile, celebrates the artistic movement that flourished in Harlem, New York, in the 1920s and '30s. And you can check out displays on robotics, lasers, and biotechnology at the Madison Science Museum, or experiment the day away at the L.R. Ingersoll Physics Museum at UW-Madison.

Wisconsin Historical Museum
30 N. Carroll St., (608) 264-6555
historicalmuseum.wisconsinhistory.org

Wisconsin Veterans Museum
30 W. Mifflin St., (608) 267-1799
wisvetsmuseum.com

Harlem Renaissance Museum
1444 E. Washington Ave., (608) 239-0921

Madison Science Museum
211 N. Carroll St., (608) 216-5496

L.R. Ingersoll Physics Museum
1150 University Ave., (608) 262-4526
physics.wisc.edu/ingersollmuseum

FIND MASTERPIECES EVERYWHERE
AT ART FAIR ON THE SQUARE

When 500 artists from around the country intersect with nearly 200,000 art lovers, it's easy to see why Art Fair on the Square has been a Madison cultural tradition for nearly 60 years. The event showcases paintings, sculpture, photography, woodwork, jewelry, and much more on the Capitol Square. Chat with artists while browsing their work, and then check out the live music and food vendors that accompany the event held by the Madison Museum of Contemporary Art. Once you've looped the Square, head west for the Emerge Block, which spotlights nearly a dozen early career artists on the 100 block of State Street, or turn east to Art Fair Off the Square, an annual showcase by the Wisconsin Alliance of Artists and Craftspeople featuring the work of more than 100 Wisconsin artists.

Art Fair on the Square and Art Fair Off the Square
are held over one weekend in July.
(608) 257-0158, mmoca.org
(608) 204-9129, artcraftwis.org

WISH UPON A STAR
AT WASHBURN OBSERVATORY

When the Washburn Observatory opened in 1881 on a hill on the UW-Madison campus overlooking Lake Mendota, it boasted a 15.6-inch refractor telescope, one of the largest in the country at the time. The domed building was a hub for research up until the 1950s, when the university constructed a new observatory west of the city. Today, the Astronomy Department holds free public open houses at Washburn throughout the year—informal events led by astronomy graduate students—that offer dazzling looks at the night sky.

The observatory is open to the public on the first and third
Wednesday of each month and every Wednesday, June through

August, weather permitting.
1401 Observatory Dr.
astro.wisc.edu

DISCOVER THE MAGIC
OF LOCAL THEATER

From professional companies to community troupes, classic works to original skits, probing drama to off-the-wall comedy, Madison's theater scene is eclectic and thriving. Forward Theater Company stages high-caliber, buzzworthy shows at Overture Center, where the revered Children's Theater of Madison also performs. Theatre LILA is consistently interesting and collaborative in its offerings, while Capital City Theatre and Four Seasons Theatre focus on musical theater. The Bartell Theatre is home base for five local theater groups, each with its own creative niche, and Broom Street Theater has been pushing boundaries and surprising audiences with original plays since 1969. Fresco Opera Theatre injects opera with doses of pop culture (think *Star Wars,* reality TV, and westerns) and even stages performances in local garages.

Forward Theater Company
forwardtheater.com

Children's Theater of Madison
ctmtheater.org

Theatre LILA
theatrelila.com

Capital City Theatre
capitalcitytheatre.org

Four Seasons Theatre
fourseasonstheatre.com

**The Bartell Theatre presents shows by the
Madison Theatre Guild, Strollers Theatre,
Mercury Players Theatre, StageQ, and Kathie
Rasmussen Women's Theatre.**
bartelltheatre.org

Broom Street Theater
bstonline.org

Fresco Opera Theatre
frescooperatheatre.com

GET SAUCY
AT THE NATIONAL MUSTARD MUSEUM

An entire museum devoted to mustard? Yes—and you're going to love it! The National Mustard Museum contains the world's largest collection of mustards and mustard memorabilia—as in nearly 6,000 mustards from all 50 states and more than 70 countries, plus hundreds of other items. Those who regard mustard as that yellow stuff that squirts out of a plastic bottle will want to spend some time at the Tasting Bar. There, choose from hundreds of mustards, from sweet to hot to tequila-spiked. Pick up your favorites in the gift shop, and consider returning on the first Saturday in August, when National Mustard Day turns the site into a party complete with live music, games, and free hot dogs. Just don't ask for ketchup!

7477 Hubbard Ave., Middleton, (608) 831-2222
mustardmuseum.com

STEP INTO THE PAST
ON A HISTORIC ARCHITECTURE
WALKING TOUR

Want to know what life was like on State Street in eras past? Ever wonder who lived in the beautiful Mansion Hill homes in the late 19th century? Wish to get up close to the local Modernist movement? The Madison Trust for Historic Preservation invites you to explore the city's past through its buildings on its Historic Architecture Walking Tours. The tours, which are held in the summer, lead through architecturally interesting neighborhoods and developments—usually on foot and sometimes by bike— and end with a complimentary coffee, beer, ice cream, or other refreshment at a nearby establishment.

Tours are held on select days from June to September.
madisonpreservation.org

SCOUR THE GALLERY SCENE

Art lovers can find exhibitions of paintings, prints, photography, and more across the city. Garver Gallery has been bringing highlights of the art world, particularly atmospheric landscapes, to downtown Madison since the 1970s. Milward Farrell Fine Art specializes in "art and craft for the 21st century," while out in pretty Paoli, Artisan Gallery represents internationally known and regional artists alike, with an eye toward innovative ceramics. Printmaking doesn't get more exciting than at Tandem Press, where artists from around the world come to push the limits of the medium. And Gallery Marzen, Drunk Lunch, the Art + Literature Laboratory, Fat City Emporium, and the Madison Public Library's Bubbler program have all spotlighted local, emerging, and thoughtful artists and brought new energy to the art scene.

Garver Gallery
18 S. Bedford St., (608) 256-6755
garvergallery.com

Milward Farrell Fine Art
2701 Monroe St., (608) 238-6501
milwardfarrellfineart.com

Artisan Gallery
6858 Paoli Rd., Paoli, (608) 845-6600
artisangal.com

Tandem Press
1743 Commercial Ave., (608) 263-3437
tandempress.wisc.edu

Gallery Marzen
2345 Atwood Ave., (608) 709-1454
gallerymarzen.com

Drunk Lunch
807 E. Johnson St., (608) 630-8401
shopdrunklunch.com

Art + Literature Laboratory
2021 Winnebago St., (608) 556-7415
artlitlab.org

Fat City Emporium
2716 Atwood Ave., (608) 442-5128
fatcityemporium.com

Madison Public Library
201 W. Mifflin St., (608) 266-6300
madisonbubbler.org

PLAY AROUND
AT THE MADISON CHILDREN'S MUSEUM

Kids have so much fun at the Madison Children's Museum that they probably don't realize how much they're learning. Playing with water, running in a giant gerbil wheel, exploring a log cabin, capturing silhouettes in the Shadow Room, solving puzzles, climbing, building, and much more spark interests in science, history, and the world around them. Youngsters can paint, sculpt, or weave a masterpiece in the art studio or greet chickens on the rooftop garden, and changing exhibitions and special events mean there's always a new reason to visit. If coming to this most environmentally friendly museum in the state makes you wish you were a kid again, be sure to check out Adult Swim, a series of after-hours events just for grown-ups.

100 N. Hamilton St., (608) 256-6445
madisonchildrensmuseum.org

TIP
On the first Wednesday night of each month, the museum opens its doors to the community free of charge.

GET ART SMART
AT THE CHAZEN

Art of nearly every style, medium, time period, and place can be found at the Chazen Museum of Art. The UW-Madison art museum, which opened in 1970 and underwent a stunning expansion in 2011, holds the second-largest collection of art in the state. More than 20,000 paintings, drawings, prints, sculptures, photographs, and decorative art pieces represent artistic flourishings from ancient times to the present day. The museum is renowned for its collections of Japanese prints, glass art, and work by Regionalist artists such as Grant Wood, Thomas Hart Benton, and John Steuart Curry (whose *Our Good Earth* painting is a must-see). You'll also find pieces by Pablo Picasso, Helen Frankenthaler, Chuck Close, and other notables, plus fascinating temporary exhibitions, tours, talks, and even concerts.

750 University Ave., (608) 263-2246
chazen.wisc.edu

CHILL OUT
AT A FARMERS' MARKET CONCERT

It's late Saturday morning. You've made the rounds of the Dane County Farmers' Market on the Capitol Square and are wondering what to do next. Here's an utterly pleasant suggestion: Stroll two blocks down State Street, enter the cool quiet of Overture Center, and take in a free organ concert from the Madison Symphony Orchestra. Everyone is welcome at these relaxed, 45-minute recitals that highlight the talents of MSO organist Samuel Hutchison or a guest performer, and of course the grand 4,040-pipe Overture concert organ. They may just lead you to the symphony's free community hymn sings, held several times a year, that combine the audience's voices with the organ's sounds, and perhaps pique your interest further to attend performances during the orchestra's mainstage season.

Held on select Saturdays in the summer.
201 State St., (608) 258-4141
madisonsymphony.org/organperformances

EXPERIENCE A MIDSUMMER NIGHT'S MAGIC
AT AMERICAN PLAYERS THEATRE

All the world may be a stage, as Shakespeare famously suggested, but there's something undoubtedly special about the one at American Players Theatre. Since opening in 1980, the Spring Green theater company has presented classic works by the Bard—plus Chekhov, Ibsen, Molière, Wilde, Shaw, and others—in its open-air Up the Hill theater. While APT added an indoor, 200-seat theater in 2009 to extend its performance season into the fall, the outdoor 1,140-seat amphitheater nestled in the woods continues to beckon as a high-culture summer day trip from Madison. Picnic on the grounds before taking your seat, where the magic of live theater somehow gets even better as the sun sets, darkness settles in, and only fireflies are left to compete with the glow of the stage.

Season runs June through November.
5950 Golf Course Rd., Spring Green, (608) 588-2361
americanplayers.org

SUPPORT ARTISTS
OF ALL ABILITIES

A number of local organizations work to ensure Madisonians with disabilities have the opportunity to make art, and that brings exciting opportunities for art aficionados. VSA Wisconsin hosts an exhibition of art made by adults and children with disabilities each spring, turning the statewide art agency's headquarters (which shows some work year-round) into a vibrant gallery. ArtWorking provides mentorship, training, and studio space for artists with cognitive disabilities and helps them start their own businesses making and selling their work, while Indigo Wings is an eclectic gallery and studio space that represents artists with disabilities. Several artists, such as Phil Porter and Romano Johnson, have launched successful careers; keep your eyes open for their colorful, exuberant work exhibited around town.

VSA Wisconsin
1709 Aberg Ave., (608) 241-2131
vsawisconsin.org

ArtWorking
1955 W. Broadway, Monona, (608) 442-5294
artworking.org

Indigo Wings
4601 Monona Dr., Monona, (608) 286-1222
indigowingsinc.com

DISCOVER A HIDDEN GEM
AT THE GEOLOGY MUSEUM

Like a dazzling crystal found inside a geode, the Geology Museum is a delightful discovery. Tucked inside Weeks Hall at UW-Madison, this museum boasts more than 120,000 geological and paleontological specimens. Check out sparkly rocks and minerals inside glass cases or glowing under blacklights in a special room, or examine fascinating fossils from Wisconsin and farther afield. And if you think the museum is old—it was established in 1848—wrap your mind around a rock containing zircon crystals that are 4.4 billion years old. Don't leave before meeting the Boaz mastodon, a composite of bones from two remains found in the 1890s in southwest Wisconsin. Explore on your own or sign up for a tour that can be tailored to anyone from kindergarteners to adults.

1215 W. Dayton St., (608) 262-2399

geologymuseum.org

FIND YOUR NEXT PAGE TURNER
AT A LOCAL BOOKSTORE

It's only natural that a brainy city like Madison boasts some pretty amazing bookstores. Since 1954, Paul's Bookstore has been luring book lovers to duck into the small State Street shop, browse its packed shelves, chat up staff, and pick up a new favorite. With roots as a feminist bookstore, A Room of One's Own is an expansive store filled with a huge range of contemporary and classic books—and a continued commitment to women's studies and LGBT subjects—as well as used books by Avol's Books. Whodunits are just part of the wide-ranging selections at the charming Mystery to Me, where you can also join a book club to find readers who share your literary interests. Bibliophiles should also check out the Wisconsin Book Festival, which organizes author events all year, plus a big four-day celebration of books each October.

Paul's Book Store
670 State St., (608) 257-2968
paulsbookstore.com

A Room of One's Own
315 W. Gorham St., (608) 257-7888
roomofonesown.com

Avol's Books
315 W. Gorham St., (608) 255-4730
avolsbooks.com

Mystery to Me
1863 Monroe St., (608) 283-9332
mysterytomebooks.com

**The Wisconsin Book Festival takes place
over four days in late October.**
wisconsinbookfestival.org

Photo Credit: Joey Reuteman

SHOPPING AND FASHION

SHOP LOCAL
ON STATE STREET

There's no predicting what treasures you'll find on State Street, the pedestrian-friendly downtown promenade where many of the city's independent boutiques are clustered. Consider Anthology your source for cards, paper goods, super-soft T-shirts, and buttons with a local, lefty attitude. Madison Modern Market carries home, travel, and office accessories in pop-y colors and streamlined shapes, and Driftless Studio specializes in nature-themed cards, toys, art, and jewelry. Little Luxuries can help you find a lovely and unique gift for anyone—friend, boss, child, or sweetheart—and the Pipefitter has been a staple for gag gifts, inappropriately funny cards, and oddball trinkets since the 1970s.

TIP
Find bargains and additional fun during the Maxwell Street Days sidewalk sales the third weekend of July. maxwellstreetdays.org

Anthology
218 State St., (608) 204-2644
anthology.typepad.com

Madison Modern Market
310 State St., (608) 257-1555
shopmadmod.com

Driftless Studio
214 State St., (608) 230-5153
driftlessstudio.com

Little Luxuries
230 State St., (608) 255-7372
littleluxuriesmadison.com

The Pipefitter
520 State St., (608) 257-2400
pipefittermadison.com

FIND ENTERTAINING TREASURES
AT ORANGE TREE IMPORTS

You could easily spend hours poking around Orange Tree Imports, a delightful gift shop that's been a staple of Monroe Street for more than 40 years. Every wall, counter, and corner is packed with interesting items to discover—from scented candles, lotions, and soaps to jewelry, greeting cards, art calendars, and kids' toys. The cookware is especially inspiring: vibrantly hued dishes, bakeware, and serving bowls, gorgeous glassware, and spatulas in every shade of the rainbow are sure to step up your cooking and entertaining game at home. Or, better yet, maybe your purchases will inspire you to enroll in one of Orange Tree's popular cooking classes.

1721 Monroe St., (608) 255-8211
orangetreeimports.com

SHOP LIKE A FASHIONISTA
AT HILLDALE

The most impeccably dressed Madisonians share a secret, and it is called Hilldale. This near-west-side shopping center received a major makeover a few years back and the results could not be more chic. Here's where to find Macy's, Michael Kors, Kate Spade, Anthropologie, Free People, Madewell, and other popular higher-end stores. But don't leave without stopping by Twigs. This locally owned boutique is the go-to source for designer fashion, offering such brands as Marc Jacobs, Rag & Bone, Diane von Furstenberg, and Citizens of Humanity. The Home Market for on-trend décor, Mes Amies for adorable dresses, and Cornblooms and Morgan's Shoes for footwear are additional locally owned shops to check out.

726 N. Midvale Blvd., (608) 238-6640
hilldale.com

DRESS LIKE A SCONNIE

Show your love for Wisconsin by dressing the part! The ultimate source for Badger gear is University Book Store, which has been hooking up UW students, faculty, and fans with all manner of red and white goods since 1894. Insignia also carries Wisconsin apparel to outfit adults and kids, while Sconnie Nation puts fresh, student-focused twists on the theme (and no wonder, as the company started in a UW dorm room). Tailgate (owned by American Eagle) gives school spirit a fashionable edge, and options extend beyond game-day threads. T-shirts touting points of local pride can be found at Anthology, while those at Zip-Dang feature graphic designs of Madison's lakes. Shirts highlighting iconic neighborhoods and parks abound at Thirty State, and the Wisconsin Historical Museum's gift shop boasts tees with humorous and historical state references.

University Book Store
711 State St., (608) 257-3784
702 N. Midvale Blvd. (at Hilldale Shopping Center),
(608) 238-8455
uwbookstore.com

Insignia
639 State St., (608) 251-0495
buckyslockerroom.com

Sconnie Nation
521 State St., (608) 661-4350
sconnie.com

Tailgate
579 State St., (608) 286-1808
ae.com

Anthology
218 State St., (608) 204-2644
anthology.typepad.com

Zip-Dang
2606 Monroe St., (608) 232-1602
zip-dang.com

Thirty State
1651 Deming Way, Middleton
(at Greenway Station)
(608) 598-9003
greenwayshopping.com

Wisconsin Historical Museum
30 N. Carroll St., (608) 264-6555
historicalmuseum.wisconsinhistory.org

BE A DIY DIVA

Sure, you could buy a cute paper garland or a rustic-chic wall hanging. But wouldn't it be more fun to make your own, especially with a gaggle of friends and a glass of wine? A handful of modern crafting companies have opened with that combination in mind. Create and decorate a reclaimed-wood sign at the Crafty Project, or let the instructors at PaintBar lead you brushstroke by brushstroke in making a masterpiece. Come to a craft party at Anthology, and leave with a decoupaged frame, paper party garland, or Scrabble tile necklace. And at Revel, learn to make high-style keychains, drink trays, bottle stoppers, and other fun accessories you won't know how you lived without.

The Crafty Project
312 N. 3rd St.
thecraftyproject.com

PaintBar
1224 Williamson St., (608) 518-3044
paint-bar.com

Anthology
218 State St., (608) 204-2644
anthology.typepad.com

Revel
107 N. Hamilton St., (608) 286-1369
revelmadison.com

SHOP WITH YOUR CONSCIENCE

A strong do-good vibe runs through Madison, and that includes the retail scene. At Change, an eco-chic boutique on Willy Street, find fashion-forward fair-trade clothing. The cozy sweaters, printed dresses, and fun accessories are all made by artisans in developing countries who are given fair wages and safe working conditions. What's more, the store, which opened in 2012, pays it forward by giving to local nonprofits serving women and children. And at two Madison outposts, Serrv sells beautiful handcrafted clothing, accessories, baskets, textiles, and gifts with a mission to lift artisans from nearly 30 countries out of poverty. Why not shop to make a difference in someone else's life?

Change
1252 Williamson St., (608) 237-2707
changeboutique.com

Serrv
2701 Monroe St., (608) 233-4438
224 State St., (608) 251-2370
serrv.org

GET IN A LATHER
AT THE SOAP OPERA

You'll never look at a bar of soap the same way after a visit to this longstanding State Street shop. Since 1972, the Soap Opera has been packed with items to make your next bath or shower an utterly pleasant experience. There are more varieties of soap than you could ever imagine, plus lotions, oils, salts, and a few rubber duckies. Even if you consider yourself all set in the bath department, pop in anyway. The staff are friendly and knowledgeable, and the lovely shop is an oasis of heavenly smells set amid the constant commotion of downtown.

319 State St., (608) 251-4051
thesoapopera.com

FIND DESIGN-MINDED GOODS
AT HATCH AND HAZEL

If you feel art is essential to a good life, if you like to support local makers, and if you believe in buying high-quality goods made in the U.S.A., you'll find kindred spirits at Hatch Art House and Hazel General Store. The sister shops on quirky-cool Willy Street are casual, creative, and welcoming spaces filled with art, jewelry, bags, graphic T-shirts, cards, and other items to bring a dose of joy to the everyday. Hatch highlights Wisconsin artists, with a corner of the eclectic gallery devoted to highlighting a different painter, printmaker, sculptor, or photographer each month, while Hazel updates the general-store concept, stocking its shelves with well-designed, American-made essentials for modern life.

Hatch Art House
1248 Williamson St., (608) 247-2775
hatcharthouse.com

Hazel General Store
1250 Williamson St., (608) 237-2776
hazelgeneralstore.com

TIP
Don't miss the EcoSquared Art Show, an exhibition of artwork made from upcycled materials, each January at Hatch.

SHOP FOR THE TOTS

A handful of children's shops and toy stores joyfully convey the magic of being a kid. Capitol Kids maintains an expertly curated selection of games, books, toys, and colorful clothes in the heart of downtown. Whoops! and Co. is a play paradise with toys galore for all ages. Playthings packs in games, puzzles, and crafts, and Tradition Market carries well-made toys and clothes high on style and nostalgia. Wild Child is the place to pick up a tie-dyed onesie—or other organic, natural, and fair-trade clothes and accessories—while Satara carries eco-conscious toys and soft-hued organic baby clothes made for cuddling.

Capitol Kids
8 S. Carroll St., (608) 280-0744
capitolkids.com

Whoops! and Co.
555 S. Midvale Blvd. #105, (608) 236-4555
whoopsandco.com

Playthings
702 N. Midvale Blvd. (at Hilldale Shopping Center),
(608) 233-2124
playthingstoystore.com

Tradition Market
1835 Parmenter St., Middleton, (608) 841-2345
tradition.market

Wild Child
1813 Monroe St., (608) 251-6445
wildchildclothes.com

Satara Home & Baby
6333 University Ave., Middleton, (608) 251-4905
satarahome.com

GET CRAFTY

Crafting is cool again and local DIY-ers have even given the humble craft fair a hip, indie-spirited makeover. Art, clothing, jewelry, ceramics, candles, and vintage items are the start of what you'll find at these community-minded events. Each November, the Craftacular and the Crafty Fair let you buy handmade holiday gifts. Come spring, the MadCity Bazaar pop-up flea market sets up shop on the near-east side. The newcomer to the craft-show crew is the Bodega, an outdoor market that adds in food carts, live music, and kids' activities. And keep your eyes open for the Black Sheep Bazaar, an alternative craft fair that crops up occasionally at a local bar.

The Crafty Fair takes place each November and sometimes also in the spring at the Goodman Community Center.
149 Waubesa St.
thecraftyfair.com

The Craftacular is held each November at the Madison Masonic Center.
301 Wisconsin Ave.
madisoncraftacular.com

MadCity Bazaar is held the first and third Saturdays from May to September in the parking lot of Trinity Lutheran Church.
1904 Winnebago St.
madcitybazaar.com

The Bodega takes place on five Thursday nights from May to September.
917 E. Mifflin St.
breesestevensfield.com/bodega

● ●

BECOME A SHARP-DRESSED MAN
AT CONTEXT

When Context opened in 2005, local men no longer had excuses for not looking as stylish as their counterparts on the East and West Coasts. The King Street shop outfits the best-dressed guys in town, carrying a wide range of denim, shirts, shoes, and more from the coolest brands around. Its staffers take denim particularly seriously, and they're happy to educate you on the importance of a well-made and great-fitting pair of jeans. *GQ* and *The New York Times* are just a few of the major pubs to sing the praises of this shop tucked quietly and confidently just steps from the Capitol Square.

113 King St., (608) 250-0113
contextclothing.com

SUGGESTED
ITINERARIES

QUINTESSENTIALLY MADISON

WISCO ESSENTIALS

BADGER PRIDE

BRING THE KIDS

FREE FUN

PHOTO OPP

GREAT OUTDOORS

GET MOVING

ACTIVITIES
BY SEASON

SPRING

Eat Local at the Dane County Farmers' Market, 2

Exhibition-Hop on Gallery Night, 46

Enjoy a Moveable Feast, 10

Get Your Ticket to the Wisconsin Film Festival, 42

Celebrate Heritage, 48

Celebrate School Spirit at the Varsity Band Concert, 41

Run like Mad at Crazylegs, 78

SUMMER

Pair Music with Food at Concerts on the Square, 36

Take to the Terrace, 60

Groove Together at Dane Dances, 43

Party in the Street at Live on King Street, 55

Score a Home Run of Fun at a Mallards Game, 70

Step into the Past on a Historic Architecture Walking Tour, 107

Find Masterpieces Everywhere at Art Fair on the Square, 102

Experience a Midsummer Night's Magic at American Players Theatre, 113

FALL

WINTER

INDEX